3 Day Guide to Berlin
A 72-hour definitive guide on what to see, eat and enjoy in Berlin, Germany

3 DAY CITY GUIDES

Copyright © 2014 BeautyBodyStyle, LLC

All rights reserved. No part of this book may be reproduced in any form or by any electronic or mechanical means including information storage and retrieval systems – except in the case of brief quotations in articles or reviews – without the permission in writing from its publisher.

Although the author and publisher have made every effort to ensure that the information in this book was correct at press time, the author and publisher do not assume and hereby disclaim any liability to any party for any loss, damage, or disruption caused by errors or omissions, whether such errors or omissions result from negligence, accident, or any other cause.

Image use under CC-BY License via Flickr

Photo Credits:
Berlin Cathedral Manuel Martín
Berlin Wall Abhijeet Rane
Kurhaus Kursakow Restaurant dean07000
Kuppel des Reichstagsgebäudes Barbara Müller-Walter

ISBN: 1505378001
ISBN-13: 978-1505378009

"I see my path, but I don't know where it leads. Not knowing where I'm going is what inspires me to travel it." – Rosalia de Castro.

CONTENTS

1	Introduction to Berlin	1
2	Berlin Neighborhoods	12
3	How to Not Get Lost in Berlin	16
4	Day 1 in Berlin	18
5	Day 2 in Berlin	26
6	Day 3 in Berlin	33
7	Where to Stay, Eat & Party	39
8	Berlin Local Cuisine	49
9	Berlin Travel Essentials	51
10	German Language Essentials	54
11	Berlin Top 20 Things to Do	61
	Conclusion	67
	More from This Author	68

1 INTRODUCTION TO BERLIN

Nikolaiviertel, Berlin. Photo credit: János Balázs via Flickr

So why Berlin?

Out of all the cities in the world, why choose this one? Berlin is a city that offers an incredible variety of experiences where everyone can find something to their liking – from art and music lovers, to social travelers and history buffs.

If you want to be captivated and spun around from

ancient history to today's bustling party scene, Berlin will not disappoint. Berlin's archeological sites date as far back as the 12th century and every era afterwards. From the Prussian Empire to Communist Germany, many places have left its mark on the city, making it a unique place to take a walk through the centuries.

With landmarks such as the Brandenburg Gate, the Ishtar Gate from Babylon, the Berlin Wall – a portrait of the divided forces in Europe and the world-renown Berlin Philharmonic. The city's electric entertainment scene serves as a counterpart to ancient history. Berlin is one of Europe's most glorious nightlife destinations, as illustrated by the success of the iconic club, Berghain.

For travelers seeking to experience a myriad of diversities, get ready to dive in. There are nearly 180 nationalities living in Berlin and every one of them has brought its own culture and uniqueness.

This rich variety has contributed to the openness of this German capital in a way that keeps tourists coming back for more. Social travelers who are looking to not only see the sights, but also meet the people, will have no problem doing so at Berlin's playful beach paradises. Here, you can play volleyball with the locals, enjoy a few beers and take in the warm rays.

Even though Germany's capital city is spread over 344.3 square miles (891.8 km²) in the European

Plain, its count of occupants comes in at barely 3.5 million. This means that unlike many major cities on the old continent, Berlin is a spacious megapolis. Moreover, it is one of Europe's greenest cities.

Numerous parks and water sources beautify the urban landscape, most famously the Tiergarten, Victriapark, Schlossgarten and Charlottenburg, among others. The river Spree twists and turns around the city, providing a great opportunity for leisurely strolls close to nature. What is more, just outside of the city many lakes can be found, perfect for a weekend trip outside of the hustle and bustle of Berlin.

This wonderful city is captivating with its grand architecture, streamed from rich history. More importantly, the historical events have shaped the face of modern Berlin. You can clearly see the difference that history has made by visiting thought-provoking monuments like the Wall Memorial.

Afterwards, a walk through Under the Linden Boulevard will carry you to one of the city's great traditional restaurants where you can end your day will a plate full of tasty Kartoffelpuffer and Apfelstrudel.

History

Berlin Wall. Photo credit: <u>LulaTaHula</u> via Flickr

Berlin, if nothing else, is a city full of history that will inevitably attract you, even if you are not so keen on knowing who reigned over what and when. In short, history buffs be prepared for the city's rich history to steal your heart away. Afterall, if you would like to truly understand the people of Berlin, understanding their history isn't a bad place to start.

Even though there is no clear evidence about the first settlements in the Berlin area, in 2012, diggings in Berlin Mitte, or the most central and oldest part of the city ("Mitte" means "middle" in German) discovered remains of wooden houses. What was left of the buildings was dated to the 12th century, or more specifically – 1174.

Berlin is not only an old city, but also an old capital and was the center of several regimes nonetheless. The first was the Kingdom of Prussia, which existed between 1701 and 1918 and included some of the territories that today belong to Germany, Russia, Poland, Lithuania, Denmark, the Check Republic and Belgium. The German Empire, or German Reich ("Reich" means "realm"), was within the Kingdom of Prussia, which existed from 1871 to the defeat in World War I in 1918.

Next, Berlin was the capital of the Weimar Republic, which was fairly short-lived, as it existed from 1919 to 1933. This was the first time Germany had a semi-presidential democracy. It was called "Weimar" after the name of the city where the constitution was drafted.

After the Weimar Republic, Berlin was capital to Nazi Germany, from 1933 to 1945, when the country and its government were mainly controlled by Adolf Hitler and his party, called the National Socialist German Workers' Party (NSDAP). Hitler and Nazi Germany were defeated by the Allied Forces in 1945, which put an end World War II in Europe. After the war, Berlin was divided into two and became the border between East and West Germany. The Berlin wall separated not only the city or the country, but the entire continent of Europe into two parts governed in severely different ways. The wall was erected in 1961 and brought down in 1989, with the fall of the Communist regime. Finally, only 24 years ago, in

1990, Berlin once again became the capital of the entire country, as Germany was reunited.

Today, Berlin is the capital of the Federal Republic of Germany and is home to 3.5 million people of more than 180 nationalities. This great diversity is one of the key characteristics of the city.

Climate

Berlin is not only diverse when it comes to historical events. Its climate is classified as temperate oceanic, which means that each season the city is utterly transformed and, depending on when you decide to visit, you are surely going to have very different experiences. The temperatures are quite varied, as they range from below 0ºC (29ºF) to more than 30ºC (86ºF). Even though Berlin normally has a lot of rainy days, snow cover during the winter does not last long. You should also know that roaming the city will provide you with a few more degrees of heat, as the buildings store it and create a microclimate of sorts, while the surrounding suburban areas are a bit cooler.

Seasons

Usually, the winters are rather cold and the summers hot, while spring and autumn offer moderation. In the coldest months, January and February, temperatures can drop below 0ºC (29ºF) and while it snows between December and March, the snow cover does not normally last long. If you enjoy the sunshine and don't mind getting a little sweaty, you might like visiting Berlin in its hottest months, July and August, when temperatures reach 30ºC (86ºF). Another thing that you should prepare for when planning your trip is the high humidity, which ranges from 60% (April - July) to 80% (November - February) and can accentuate the temperatures, making the weather conditions a bit more difficult to handle. If you are meticulous when it comes to your hair and fight with everything you have to keep the frizz away, you might want to consider not only the humidity, but the precipitation as well. It is always a good idea to carry an umbrella or even a raincoat in Berlin, as the average rainfall ranges from 35 mm (1.377 inches) usually in February and March, to 72 mm (2.953) in July.

Best time to visit

The best time to visit the city is spring and winter. During the spring, the weather is moderate and so you will be able to walk around all day without getting too cold or too hot. Besides, spring is when Berlin is in bloom – walking down the Under the Linder Boulevard or the Tiergarten will take you to a fairytale world of newly sprouted leaves and scantly flowers. Winters in Berlin can get frosty, but the Christmas markets are a wonderful way to escape the chill. They can be found all around the city, with brightly-lit tents, offering delicious Gluhwein (hot wine with herbs and fruit) that will warm you up.

Language

The two official languages spoken in Berlin are German and English. Even though most Germans speak English, you will bring happy smiles to the locals' faces if you try asking them for directions in German, or at least greet and part with German expressions. About 95% of the population in Berlin speaks German, though you can hear many accents because of the wide range of nationalities living in the city.

Getting In

Because of Germany's prior separation, most airports, bus and train stations were built either in East or West Berlin. Still, since the reunification all entrances to the city can be used, which makes it a very comfortable access point from all over the world.

By plane

The city's main airport is Tegel International, located in the north-west part of Berlin. Most large, international companies land and board from there and so do some domestic flights.

Schönefeld is where most you will land if you have boarded a low-cost flight, a charter, as well as some of the flights from Eastern Europe. This used to be the main GDR airport.

By train

The train companies that allow access to Berlin are ICE, InterCity EuroCity and the national Deutsche Bahn. You can travel with a train to Berlin from most European cities and even from Asia. Just make sure to make reservations ahead of time, as seats usually get booked very fast.

By bus

The Central Bus Station is located in the Charlottenburg borough. Buses from over 350 destinations in Europe travel to Berlin.

By car

The city is enclosed by a motorway ring, from which you can take a few motorways directly leading to the city – A111, A114, A113, A115, B96 and B105 are the main ones.

Getting Around

Complementing the city's green landscape, Berlin has one of the lowest numbers of cars per capita in comparison with most European cities. There are many greener, cheaper and more practical ways to get around the city. Using these means of transportation is made easy by the readily available English instructions.

Berlin's public transport system truly lives up to the stereotype that Germany is meticulously organized. The network is divided into three parts – A (the most central part of Berlin), B (just out of the city's immediate center) and C (the outer parts of Berlin). In short, this means that your travel around the city has been made very convenient.

The city offers a few cards which combine unlimited access to public transport and discount to a lot of museums, theatres and attractions. For tram travel, you can purchase a 72-hour pass, called the WelcomeCard – it costs 24,40 € and with it you can use the U-Bahn and S-Bahn within zones A and B. An alternative is the three-zone card, which costs 2 € more, but allows you to travel to the Berlin Schoenefeld airport as well as the Prussian Palaces and Gardens.

Are you keen to visit the Pergamon Museum and the gate to Babylon? Then you might find another pass useful – the WelcomeCard Berlin Museum Island. It is available in two forms – one that covers zones A and B (34 €) and another that covers all three zones (36 €). Whichever one you decide to go with, this card includes entry to the establishments of Museum Island in central Berlin.

Single tickets are another option - a ticket for zones A and B costs 2,60 €, for B and C – 2.90 € and for the three zones – 3. 20 €. Tickets can be purchased from your bus driver, machines at the entrance of stations, as well as bus and tram platforms. Every machine has English instructions so it is easy to use. Remember to validate your machine-bought tickets. Additionally, remember that Berlin has ticket controllers that will fine you if you are travelling without a ticket.

You can purchase a Berlin WelcomeCard online, at this address: http://www.berlin-welcomecard.de/en

2: BERLIN NEIGHBORHOODS

Berlin is one of the largest capitals in Europe, about four times the size of Paris. Berlin is divided into 12 districts, or Bezirks, as the Germans call them. These districts also have some sub-districts or officially recognized localities. The districts of Berlin are Charlottenburg-Willmersdorf, Friedrichshain-Kreuzberg, Lichtenberg, Marzahn-Hellersdorf, Mitte, Neukölln, Pankow, Reinickendorf, Spandau, Steglitz-Zehlendorf, Tempelhof-Schöneberg and Treptow-Köpenick.

Charlottenburg-Willmersdorf covers the western area of Berlin. It is a family friendly neighborhood that favors upscale living. With its 5 star restaurants and museums, tourists are quickly lured into this part of the city.

Friedrichshain-Kreuzberg stretches across both sides of the river. It is a central urban district with a vibrant hipster scene, cool bars and street art. Other highlights include Landwehr Canal, the beautiful street of Bergmannstasse, Neun market hall and the popular square, Boxhagener Platz.

Lichtenberg is another district in Berlin that is

close to the center where luxurious villas and residences can be found. It is a fantastic mix of modern and old architecture and urban dwellings.

Marzahn-Hellersdorf is an area where you can find both modern buildings and those built centuries ago. This, coupled with its greenery, makes it one of the more interesting districts of Berlin.

Mitte is a district in the center of Berlin full of landmarks, monuments, stunning buildings, cafes, restaurants and shopping centers. It is the district in which most visitors begin their exploration of Berlin as it houses Alexanderplatz, the TV tower and Museum Island.

Neukölln is known as the Bohemian village of Berlin with museums, an opera house, theatre, Turkish markets, underground clubs and dive bars. There is also Britz Castle whose gardens that attract many visitors.

Pankow is famous for its 19th century architecture, numerous bars and cafes and a vibrant cultural scene. Here you will find art galleries, hip designer boutiques and organic eats. Nightlife here also hums with life, but for those who like peace and quiet, there are rural areas perfect for recreation.

Reinickendorf is a district with 10 sub-districts, but not many residents. It is a peaceful place, full of greenery, with charming lakes and rural areas. It is located on the north-west of Berlin.

Spandau is full of history and is located in the old quarter of the city. Here you will find a great number of historical buildings that have stood for centuries. Spandau also contains fields, forests and country sides that make it a diverse and inviting area.

Steglitz-Zehlendorf is a district located in the south-west of the Berlin. It is easy accessible and other areas of the Berlin can be reached in no time from this district. It is also diverse like Spandau, with both urban and rural surroundings.

Tempelhof-Schöneberg Tempelhof is the industrial area of Berlin; some of the well-known corporations and institutions are located right in this part of the city. In contrast, Schöneberg is a beautiful area filled with green spaces namely Gleisdreick Park and a thriving selection of local restaurants and bars.

Treptow-Köpenick is located only a few minutes away from the center, on the south-east side of Berlin. It has a lot of greenery, parks and rivers where you can relax, but it also has the urban side where you can find restaurants, bars, cafes and clubs with great nightlife.

Walking Tours

One of the best walking tours in Berlin is the **SANDEMANs Free Tour** where you will get a chance to see the most important sites in the city: http://www.newberlintours.com/daily-tours/free-tour.html Another great tour is the **Original Berlin Walks** that focuses mostly on the history and culture of Berlin: http://www.berlinwalks.de/public/

3: HOW TO NOT GET LOST IN BERLIN

Berlin is one of the largest cities in Europe and with key attractions scattered throughout the city, its not difficult to find yourself lost. However in every city, including Berlin, there are key landmarks and signs to help determine where you are and how get back on track.

Using public transportation, especially those who are visiting Berlin for the first time, is a great way to orient yourself to the city. The designated routes and maps within the stations aid travellers in efficiently keeping a pulse on their location.

Most visitors begin their exploration of the Berlin from the Brandenburg Gate, which is located in the heart of Berlin. It is also the starting point of the Eastern Berlin and its most famous street Unter dem Linden. The Royal Palace, another useful landmark is located at the opposite end of this street. In addition, this street also houses Museum Island, a complex of museums built by the Royal family.

If you head to the *opposite* side of the Brandenburg

Gate, along the Strasse des 17 Juni, you will reach the city's largest park, Tiergarten. Should you arrive reach Tiergarten from the opposite side of the park, follow Strasse des 17 Juni and you will reach the center of Berlin.

The Berlin wall, or the remains of it, located in Eastern Berlin is another great orientation point that will let know if you are on the west or east side of the city. An alternative method to determine if you are in the west or east side of Berlin are the unique traffic lights. Ampelmann, or the traffic lights for the pedestrians, are represented as a man with a hat and can be only found in East Berlin.

From almost every sector of Berlin, except outside the city, you can see the TV Tower which is 207m high, making it the highest building in Berlin. Navigate the streets towards this tower and when you reach it, you will find yourself at Alexanderplatz from where you can easily find your way by foot or using public transportation. The TV Tower also features a tourist info center.

There are several tourists info centers scattered throughout Berlin that typically operate between the hours of 9.30am-6.00pm. Remember Brandenburg Gate? There is a prominent tourist info center located within its south wing. If you are in West Berlin, you will find another key tourist info center within the walls of the Europe Center, the city's largest shopping center. Hours at this location are between 10.00am-8.00pm, Monday-Saturday.

4 DAY 1 IN BERLIN

Day 1

The boulevard Unter den Linden with the Guard House. Photo Credit: Blepo

Under the Linden Boulevard: This is a beautiful way to begin your tour around Berlin. The boulevard has both car and pedestrian areas, though the latter are better for a picturesque impression of the city. Setting foot the boulevard, you will see a very long, neatly paved lane. The boulevard is large and wide, so walking down it is never a hassle, despite the large numbers of tourists and locals. The linden trees on both sides of the lane branch out to decorate the lane. They even form green tunnels at times and are skilfully trimmed.

Even in the winter, when the leaves have fallen out, the boulevard has unique charm. At that time of year, the trees are covered in snow and glowing lights. Walking down the boulevard at night is a real treat – there aren't as many people and the alley is always brightly lit in color. A stroll down this beautiful boulevard is an effortless way to step into the magnificence of the city. You will be able to meet firsthand the famous diversity of Berlin – tourists, children playing, local couples holding hands and mothers with strollers, will help you experience the laid-back side of Berlin.

For your first stroll around the city, you can start at the intersection with Shinkelplatz and the river Spree. This way you would be able to take a quick look at Berlin's most famous and important river. If you want to experience a bit of old-time luxury, you can have a cup of coffee at the The Einstein Unter den Linden. This is the most famous café in the district and is often preferred by politicians and media representatives. If you would prefer something simpler, you can always grab a cup of cappuccino or strong Americano from one of the street vendors. Combining it with a traditional snack, such as the pretzel or Apfelstruddel will contribute to your Berlin experience.

Opening hours: always open

Admission fee: none

Suggested arrival time: 9 am

DDR Museum: The Linden Boulevard will take you to your first stop on this journey of Berlin – a museum unlike anything you have seen. This museum is a wonderful way to understand the era of Communist Germany and, more specifically, the culture of East Germany. You will be transported back to over 25 years ago, and will be able see all the technological advancements of this time. This is an exceptional opportunity to experience the way people lived back then. You will feel as though you have boarded a time-machine and have been transported right to the GDR (German Democratic Republic or East Germany).

This is not your regular museum with boring exhibitions behind glass. The DDR Museum is an interactive place, where you are encouraged to touch and poke all the exhibits. You will not only see, but rather experience life in the GDR. For instance, you can enter a living room with a homely feel, sit on the couch, open the cupboards and explore all the utensils used at the time.

Opening hours: Monday – Sunday 10am - 8pm; Saturday 10am - 10pm

Admission fee: Regular - €6; Groups - €4

Suggested arrival time: 9:30 am

Berlin Television Tower: Or in German – Fernsehturm, is one of the city's most important landmarks – it holds the tallest observation deck in Berlin and was designed as a symbol of the city and GDR architecture. Even though the queues are usually rather long and you will spend about 30 minutes to an hour and a half waiting, the view from the top is worth it. If you have decided to visit Berlin in the winter you might not have to wait as much, but still it would be better to arm yourself with patience.

Another way to beat the queues is buy a VIP ticket online. The Berlin TV Tower is a good place to get a realistic first impression of the city's caliber and magnificence. The tower allows you take a 360° trip around Berlin, giving you an eagle's eye view of the city layout and what you are about to explore. The tower has observation decks at two levels – 203 and 207 meters (666, and 678 feet).The Berlin TV Tower took 4 years to construct (1965-1969) and is a prominent symbol of Berlin. It dominates the skyline with its 368 meters (1207 feet). An interesting fact is that when the sun shines over the tower, the reflection resembles a cross. That is how it became known as "The Pope's Revenge" – at the time of its construction the church was disregarded in East Germany.

Opening hours: March to October: 9 a.m. – 12 p.m. ; November to February: 10 a.m. 12 p.m.

Admission fee: Regular - €13; VIP - €23

You can purchase tickets online here: http://tv-turm.de/en/online-tickets.php

Suggested arrival time: 11:30

Alexanderplatz: Or Alex, as Berlin locals affectionately call it, is one of the most central squares in the city. It used to be in East Germany and the architecture really gives that away. The square is home to large concrete structures, with clean lines and a mechanical feel. It is a spacious place, covered mostly in concrete and steel, but it is also an important part of Berlin's heritage. This landmark has a long history, dating back to the Prussian Kingdom, when it was used as a cattle market. Later, in 1805 it was names Alexanderplatz after the Russian Emperor Alexander I. Perhaps the most distinctive feature of Alex, is its large clock, showing the time of several places in the world. It was built during the GDR era, as a technological advancement.

Near Alex is a large department store, where you could do some shopping. There are also many restaurants and cafes, as well as a bus and tram terminal. Don't be surprised to see people base-jumping from the roof of the nearby Park Inn.

Alkopole is a cozy little bar and dinner establishment, located right on Alexanderplatz. You can sit down for some tasty German Wurst and a salad, along with traditional beer.

Opening hours: always open

Admission fee: none

Suggested arrival time: 12:30 am

Berlin Underworld: A good place to get away from the busy tourist attractions is to visit the Berlin Underworld of bunkers. In Gesundbrunnen Underground railway station you will find a green door that many overlook. However, if you prefer places off the beaten path, you will certainly enjoy the treasure, hidden behind that door.

The non-profit Unterwelten (underworld) society organizes tours, which will allow you to peek into the myriad of tunnels and bunkers, an important part of living in the DDR. The tunnels were left untouched after the Berlin Wall was erected and so their original atmosphere has been preserved. You can really sense the dire reality of what it was like to spend time in this cold, claustrophobic maze with the threatening roar of bomber aircraft above. The bunkers were a key part of civilian life in East Germany. Over 1,000 living spaces were being used in the 1940s, all connected with a complex network of tunnels. Reliving the events of World War II and the eerie safety that the tunnels provided is made possible with Berlin Underworld. The only way you can visit this attraction is by taking part of a tour. Please note that children under age 7 are not permitted.

Opening hours:

Tours from April 4th to October 31st, Thursday,

Saturday, Monday, Tuesday at 3 pm.

Admission fee: €11

Suggested arrival time: 2:30 pm

Berlin Wall Memorial: This landmark is a must-see in Berlin. The Wall Memorial-allows you to witness in person everything you have read about or seen in movies. The Nazi era, all the terror and suffering that people experienced during that time, are made comprehensive to the visitors by a wide range of displays. You can read about the formation of Germany's division, as well as the way it affected the country's people. Your passion for man-made structures will be elevated to a whole new level, by seeing how a simple construction of concrete and steel can affect the lives of millions. This is the last piece of the dividing wall, with the grounds behind it preserved as well. Visiting this place transports you back to the Nazi times and helps you understand the division of Germany. This piece of wall separated an entire continent in two, parted families and changed people's lives forever. All of the displays have been translated to English, so diving into history is made easy.

The Documentation Center is a part of the monument, and is scheduled to reopen after reconstruction on November 9, 2014, at the anniversary of the wall's fall. The exhibition center will hold a historical overview of the most important events before and after the wall was erected. The Chapel of Reconciliation is also here – a historical place of prayer and hope, still holding some of the original elements of the Church of Reconciliation. In the Nordbahnhof S-Bahn is an exhibition that tells the story of Germany's previously heavily guarded train-station, where only trains from the West could enter.

Opening hours:

Documentation Center:

April – October - Tuesday - Sunday 9:30am – 7:00pm

November – March - Tuesday - Sunday 9:30am - 6:00pm

Open-air exhibition and memorial:

All year round Monday - Sunday 8:00am - 10:00pm

Admission fee: none

Suggested arrival time: 6:00 pm

5 DAY 2 IN BERLIN

Day 2

Berlin Cathedral. Photo credit: Manuel Martín via Flickr

Berlin Cathedral: You can start your second day of adventuring in Berlin at the Mitte borough, once again. This is always a good place to start, because it is the centermost location in Berlin and. For your second day, you can begin at the Berlin Cathedral, which is short for Supreme Parish and Collegiate Church. The dramatic, neo-Renaissance building is an iconic part of Berlin by no coincidence.

The church's construction was completed in 1905. Even though it is known as a cathedral, it has never been the seat of a bishop and so it is actually just a church. Nevertheless, both the interior and exterior are heavily ornamented with detailed handiwork. The inside of the Berlin Cathedral combines white walls and dark wood benches and alters. The gilded embellishments are the final touch. You don't have to be religious to appreciate the beauty and refinement of this building. Still, you could appreciate the façade from the small park outside. It is a place for locals and tourists alike to enjoy sunny days.

Opening hours:

Monday – Saturday: 9:00 am – 8:00 pm

Sunday: 12:00 am – 8:00 pm

Admission fee: €7

Suggested arrival time: 9:00 am

Museum Island: From the Berlin Cathedral, you can go to Under the Linden Boulevard, see the river and walk along its bank until you reach Museum Island. This is a UNESCO World Heritage Site and is located within two branches of the Spree. Museum Island is home to the Altes Museum, oldest one in Berlin, the Neues Museum, the Old National Gallery, Bode Museum and Pergamon

Museum. Touring all the museum requires at least a day, but if your time is limited you can see the two most famous ones - <u>Pergamon Museum</u> and <u>Neues Museum</u>.

The first is perhaps one of the very best places in the world to discover the mysteries of ancient civilizations. If you want to know exactly how they lived, prospered and eventually disappeared, Pergamont Museum offers elaborate displays. The exhibits are incredibly well preserved and there are detailed audio guides that you can utilize. Everything in this museum is arranged so that it tells the tale of ancient civilizations in a comprehensive way. Two of the most important exhibits are the Ishtar Gate, which was the 8th gate to the city of Babylon, and the large alter of Zeus. The alter is one of the oldest, dating back to the 2nd century BC.

Neues Museum holds one of Europe's most extensive Egyptian collections. You will experience the ancient world of pharaohs, walking among well-preserved and reconstructed pillars, statues and artifacts.

Opening hours:

Monday – Sunday: 10:00 am – 6:00 pm

Admission fee: €18

Suggested arrival time: 10:00 am

Bebelplatz: After the museums, you could either go back to Under the Linden Boulevard, or take to the small alleys on your way to Bebelplatz square. This is large, paved space, holding a lot of history and interesting stories. Sitting on the square and observing the buildings around is a special experience. Bebelplatz holds some of the most elegant architectural works of Berlin. This is where you will find the State Opera house, especially beautiful in the evenings, when it is lit.

Another impressive building on the square is the Humboldt University, which was founded in 1810 as the University of Berlin. The building has a grand stone façade, though not too ornamented. The last remarkable building on the square is <u>St. Hedwig's Cathedral</u> - the first church built in Prussia after the Reformation. The square itself is an important site. Here, in 1933, the Nazi book-burning ceremonies were held. To mark the event, there is a row of empty shelves which you can see through a window in the pavement. Looking through the window is a way to experience the cultural devastation the burnings have caused.

Opening hours: none

Admission fee: none

Suggested arrival time: 1:30 pm

Gendarmenmarkt: Your can continue your stroll around Berlin by visiting Gendarmenmarkt next. Here you can find a great place for some lunch and relaxation. Visit Bistro am Gendarmenmarkt, to enjoy some wine or beer, along with Berliner currywurst and mushroom soup.

This is one of the most important squares in the city. It is home to some of the most famous and visited landmarks in Berlin, such as the sculpture of German poet <u>Friedrich Schiller</u>. Furthermore, this square offers architectural magnificence in the face of Konzerthaus, which is home of the famous Berlin Orchestra, as well as the French and German cathedrals. A night stroll of this place offers a gorgeous display of lights. At winter time the square holds the most charming Christmas Market, where you can enjoy typical German snacks, such as Apfellstrudel, as well as gluhwein – hot wine with fruit and herbs. Visiting the Christmas market on Gandermarkt square, you will experience the real German holiday spirit- cheerful, bright and delicious.

Opening hours: none

Admission fee: none

Suggested arrival time: 2:30 pm

East Side Gallery: The next part of the itinerary will take you a bit further from the city center, but is worth it. This is a great place for art lovers to appreciate contemporary crafts. The East Side Gallery, which is a 1.3 km (0.81 miles) part of the former Berlin wall, has given new life to a glum place. The exhibition is an atypical display of colorful and even humorous depictions of social issues in Germany and Europe. It is one of the most iconic places in Berlin, as it holds the city's spirit of diversity. In 1990 artists from all over the world were invited to become part of the wall's transformation. The theme was "freedom", which was an especially important issue right after the reunification of Germany. Currently, the wall is home to 105 unique paintings with a political message of freedom. Visiting the gallery in the afternoon light elicits the colors and makes the murals even more beautiful.

Opening hours: none

Admission fee: none

Suggested arrival time: 5:00 pm

Berlin Skate Hall: At the end of the day, why not off the beaten path? You will encounter few tourists, if any, and will see a different side of Berlin.

Close to the East Side Gallery, you can find the Berlin Skate Hall. This is a world-famous spot for skaters and BMX riders to showcase their skills. The center attraction is the large half pipe. People new to the sport are also encouraged to give it a try. There a professional instructors at the Skate Hall, so you can safely skate with their help.

Opening hours:

Tuesday – Saturday: 2:00pm – 12:00 am

Monday and Sunday: 1:00 pm – 8:00 pm

Admission fee: none

Suggested arrival time: 7:00 pm

6 DAY 3 IN BERLIN

Day 3

Brandenburg Gate at night. Photo credit: <u>Francisco Antunes</u> via Flickr

Brandenburg Gate: Today you can start at the end of Under the Linden Boulevard – at the Brandenburg Gate. It was built as a monument of peace, by King <u>Frederick William II of Prussia</u>. Unfortunately, during the bombings in World War II, the Brandenburg Gate sustained serious damage. In 2002 it was restored back to its former appearance and now you can enjoy it just like the Prussians did. During the time of the DDR, the Brandenburg Gate stood right in the middle between East and West Germany. This was one of the key dividing points of Europe. The gate looks majestic, with its six towering stone pillars. On top is a large metal quadriga – a Roman chariot drawn by four horses. In front of the gate is the Paris Square. The landmark's name was chosen to honor the anti-Napolen Allies. This is a great place to sit down and watch the world go by as tourists and local alike fill the square.

Opening hours: always open

Admission fee: none

Suggested arrival time: 9:00 am

Reichstag building: Just a block away from the Brandenburg Gate is the Reichstag building. This impressively large structure was erected as home to the Imperial Diet, or the Parliament of the German Empire. However, by the end of World War II, the building was rendered obsolete and was deserted. This led to the façade's deterioration, until it was renovated in 1990.

Today, the Reichstag building once again houses the German parliament. With the restoration, a new structure was added to the building. At the top of the construction, lays a glass dome that people like to visit for the 3600 view of the city, though you can also peek into the main hall of the parliament from there. The glass dome has become more popular with tourists, than the Reichstag itself. It is a large, contemporary structure that overlooks most of Berlin. There is also a rooftop restaurant – Feinkost Kaefer, where you can enjoy brunch and a drink, while admiring the view. The tour could end with a few relaxing moments on the meadow next to the building. This is a great place for the social traveler, as you can meet many locals and tourists from around the world.

Opening hours:

November – March: 8:00 am – 6:00 pm

April – October: 8:00 am – 8:00 pm

Admission fee: none; reservation is required, you can do it at https://visite.bundestag.de/BAPWeb/pages/creat eBookingRequest.jsf?lang=en

Suggested arrival time: 11:00 am

Holocaust Memorial: While the Reichstag building is on one side of the Brandenburg Gate, the Holocaust Memorial is on the other. This is a memorial to the killed in Europe, during Nazi rule. This is one of Berlin's key landmarks, as it depicts a tragic, yet important part of German history.

This impressive memorial is divided into two parts

– the stelae over the ground and the underground museum. The stelae (large concrete blocks) is 2.38 m (7 .10 feet) long and is a sculpture that is meant to induce an uneasy feeling of confusion. The best way to absorb the atmosphere is to walk the length of the stelae by yourself. This way you will be able to experience the uneasiness and empathy that the sculpture is intended to trigger. The underground museum, on the other hand, holds the personal stories of the victims. The tales are incredibly detailed and described in a very captivating manner. Please keep in mind, that the museum does not permit entrance to children under the age of 14, due to the graphic content of the exhibition.

Opening hours:

Stelae: always open

Museum: October – March : 10 am. – 7:00 pm
April – September: 10:00 am. – 8:00pm

Admission fee: none

Suggested arrival time: 1:00 pm

Tiergarten : After the Holocaust Memorial, the Tiergarten park, offers green paradise relaxation. The Großer Tiergarten (Großer means "large", but it is more often called simply Tiergarten) is a large green space in the center of Berlin. It is a favorite for locals and tourists alike. Even though Berlin is a rather green city, with a lot of vegetation even in urban areas, the Tiergarten park is lovingly called "the lungs of Berlin", because of its rich flora that filters urban air.

This is the second-largest public park in Germany, with its 210 hectares (520 acres). The park offers many recreational experiences, from bird-watching to boat-riding. Next to the park is the Victory Column, built in honor of the Prussia's triumph in the Danish-Prussian War of 1864. The column, a famous landmark, is the base for a gilded statue. The monument is of the Roman goddess of war conquest – Victoria.

Opening hours: always open

Admission fee: none

Suggested arrival time: 2:30 pm

Beach Park 61: Another great place to relax, away from the tourists, is Berlin's urban beach. This is a laid-back place, preferred by the younger locals. You can play beach volleyball, get a tan and have typical German beer in the small outdoor bar. The park is located in the trendy Kreuzberg borough, which is a very good spot – not too far from the city center, yet not in the regular attraction circuit. Here, you will experience the spirit or Berlin and will be able to freely meet a lot of open-minded people.

Opening hours: April- September

Monday – Friday: 2:00 pm – 10:00 pm

Saturday and Sunday: 10:00 am – 10:00 pm

Admission fee: €3

Suggested arrival time: 2:30 pm

Berliner Philharmonie: This is one of Berlin's most famous and places. It is a futuristic looking concert hall, just on the edge of the Tiergarten. The place is home to one of the greatest orchestras in the world – the Berlin Philharmonic. Here you can enjoy skilled performances of some of history's grandest pieces. Classical music is brought to another level with the world-renown Philharmonic. This is one of the truly best ways to remember to Berlin – all the awe-inspiring landmarks, rich history and culture, with the sound track of the Philharmonic.

Opening hours:

Monday – Friday: 3:00 pm – 6:00 pm

Saturday and Sunday: 11:00 am – 2:00 am

Admission fee: depending on the concert

You can find the performance calendar here:

http://www.berliner-philharmoniker.de/en/concerts/calendar/

Suggested arrival time: 4:00 pm

7 WHERE TO STAY, EAT & PARTY

Feinkost Käfer, Berlin. Photo credit: Tammi L. Coles via Flickr

Are you a lavish hotel kind of person or someone who likes to wing it and just spread their tent wherever? Do you prefer your meals to consist of foamy cappuccinos and fruit, or are you looking to eat your entire family's weight in the typical German Bratwrust sausages? Are you an insane party machine that can go all night, or do you prefer chilling out with a cocktail in hand?

Whatever your desires may be, Berlin will satisfy them! This diverse city has something for everyone and will not disappoint.

Where to stay

Regent Berlin – This is, by far, one of Berlin's most central and exquisite hotels. The façade does not give away much of the glamour, but the central location and posh interior tell an entirely different story. If what you are looking for is divine luxury, with a baroque feel, then you may have found your new German pad. Gourmet food, marble bathrooms and a deluxe spa center are some of the features that this 5-star hotel offers.

- *Charlottenstraße 49, 10117 Berlin, Germany*
- *+49 30 20338*

Ramada Hotel Berlin-Alexanderplatz– This 4-star hotel is located just a short walk away from some of Berlin's most popular landmarks. It is a new and very large establishment, with clean lines and brightly lit rooms. Visitors of this hotel are mostly impressed by its location and cleanliness.

- *Karl-Liebknecht-Straße 32, Berlin, Germany*
- *+49 30 30104110*

Monbijou Hotel – Located in very close proximity to Berlin's Museum Island, this 3-star boutique hotel offers its quests a stylish, serene atmosphere and a vintage British décor. Even though the rooms are slightly on the small side, visitors usually enjoy the location, interesting design and the meals offered in the hotel.

- *Monbijouplatz 1, 10178 Berlin, Germany*
- *+49 30 61620300*

Ibis Styles Hotel Berlin Mitte – Despite its 2 stars and an exterior that looks quite regular, this hotel has captured the essence of Berlin's artistic spirit. The walls are full of colorful graffiti and the rooms – bright, contemporary and edgy. Even though the hotel is located in the central area, the rooms are quite and if you are looking for a hearty breakfast you won't be disappointed.

- *Brunnenstraße 1-2, 10119 Berlin, Germany*
- *+49 30 4849110*

Cityhostel Berlin – This is one of Berlin's most popular hostels and is preferred not only by backpackers on a budget, but also by some businessmen looking for a presentation venue. The interior of this 1 star establishment is clean and simple, but you'll be able to sunbathe or play some pool with your travel companions.

- *Glinkastraße 5, 10117 Berlin, Germany*
- *+49 30 238866850*

Three Little Pigs Hostel Berlin– This charming 1

star hostel gives off a college vibe, in the best way possible, with its eatery and wood panel walls. The brick building that houses the hostel is impressive in itself and the rooms are relatively spacious.

- *Stresemannstraße 66, 10963 Berlin, Germany*
- *+49 30 26395880*

Scube Park Columbia Berlin– Even though this is a camping ground, where you can enjoy yourself among nature, the 1-star establishment is pretty much in the city center. The cabins that you will get to sleep in have one glass wall (don't worry there is a curtain too), which is a dream come true for many nature lovers. Keep in mind that the showers and bathrooms are not in the cabins.

- *Columbiadamm 160, 10965 Berlin, Germany*
- *+49 30 69807841*

Where to eat

On a budget

Cafe Krone – This unpretentious eatery has a very authentic vibe that can best be described as retro meets modern day German style. It is not so much a restaurant, as it is a bakery and coffee shop, but it serves typical German and Western European snacks and drinks. Having a classic German breakfast here, will certainly make for a pleasant start of the day, especially if you are in Berlin during the sunny months and are able to enjoy the outside tables.

- *Oderberger Straße 38, 10435 Berlin, Germany*

- *+49 30 44312221*

Alkopole – This is considered one of Berlin's gems, in terms of restaurants. It is a very small beer bar that also offers dishes, such as various types of wurst, that go well with the drink. The interior is homely and cozy, and the German beer is abundant. Alkopole is a wonderful place to watch a game with friends and experience the life of locals. The interior reminds of October fest and the mugs are sizable.

- *Alexanderplatz, 10178 Berlin, Germany*

- *+49 30 24729970*

Bistro am Gendarmenmarkt – A wonderful little venue in the heart of Berlin, offering warm ambience and tasty meals. This bistro has a retro vibe and setting foot inside is like stepping into a time-machine. The interior is classical, with polished wood and white tablecloths. There is only a small sign outside, indicating the presence of this cozy restaurant, but walking away would be a mistake. Here you can have delicious German beer and dishes, such as the famous Berliner currywurst. Moreover, the bistro, which also has outside tables, offers a combination of elegance and budget-friendliness.

- *Markgrafenstrasse 41, Berlin, Germany*
- *+49 30 204 15 01*

Medium-priced

Dicke Wirtin – This typical German bar and dinner venue is a bit farther from the city center and the main attractions, but it is one of the best places to feat on traditional German food and choose your drink from a wide variety of local beer. The interior is mostly polished wood, while the walls are covered in paintings and retro beer advertisements. This is a place equally suitable for a group of friends and a family dinner. There is outdoor sitting as well.

- *Carmerstrasse 9, 10623 Berlin, Germany*
- *+49 30 3124952*

Marjellchen – One of the best places to not only feel, but actually taste Berlin. This small restaurant is a favorite of not only tourists, but locals as well and it is famous for its authentic German meals and great beer. The atmosphere is very homely and so is the food.

- *Mommsenstraße 9, 10629 Berlin, Germany*
- *+49 30 8832676*

The high end

Bieberbau, located on Durlacher Str. 15 – This exclusive restaurant might be a tad challenging to find if you are new to Berlin, but it is definitely worth it. People from all over the world come for Bieberbau's elegant and take on typical German food. The interior is rustic, but not at all stuffy, every course if memorable and the recommended wines really complement the food.

- *Durlacher Straße 15, 10715 Berlin, Germany*
- *+49 30 8532390*

Feinkost Kaefer – This is one of the best places in Berlin for a luxurious meal with a great view. No other venue offers the exquisite elegance of this restaurant, with its snow white tables and meticulous service. Feinkost Kaefer is located in the glass dome of the Reichstag building – one of the must-see locations in Berlin. From the tome of the dome, where the restaurant is, you can see the rooftops of the entire city and some of the landmarks. Here, you can enjoy both German and French cuisine, with a specific selection menu for each time of day.

- *Platz der Republik, Reichstag Glass Dome, Berlin, Germany*
- *+49 30 2061350*

What about the party?

Are you wondering how to complete your experience after a wonderful day of sightseeing? The Berlin club scene is one worth visiting, as it is very diverse and can range from small, literally underground venues, posh and luxurious places. Generally speaking, Berlin nightlife is not particularly expensive and the party continues until morning, so you are pretty much guaranteed to have a great time. Just keep in mind that door policy can be a bit on the strict side at times, so smile as much as you can and try to put your knowledge of German to work.

On a budget

R.A.W. Temple– This is a rather small venue, but very artistic with a wonderful mixture of people and styles. It is an underground club in Berlin's former industrial area, where you can find some other clubs as well. This is a place where you will mix with the locals and will get to feel the authentic nightlife atmosphere of Berlin, while listening mainly to techno and house music.

- *Revaler Straße 99, 10245 Berlin, Germany*
- *+49 30 2924695*

Medium-priced

Watergate– Depending on the night and what kind of a party they are having, the entrance fee can vary. The club is separated into two floors, usually with more popular DJs on the second one, while the up and coming artists are on the ground level. As the club overlooks the river, enjoying the sunset at dawn is a fantastic way to end your night of drum&bass, techno and house music.

- *Falckensteinstraße 49, 10997 Berlin, Germany*
- *+49 30 61280394*

Weekend– One of Berlin's most central and popular clubs, Weekend is located on the 12th and 15th floor of the Haus Des Reisens building and has a rooftop bar as well. This is the ideal venue for dancing to some great beats while admiring the city's night lights.

- *Alexanderstraße 7, 10178 Berlin, Germany*
- *+49 30 24631676*

The high end

Berghain – This is a club unique to Berlin and is a must for everyone who has a passion for electronic music. The venue – a converted power station, looks cold and unwelcoming from the outside, but the inside holds one of Europe's most iconic clubs. It has two floors, with the second one holding a Panorama bar, where you can relax a bit and marvel in everything that this club combines – it is very liberal, artistic and at times can get downright insane, a combination that has made this club world-famous.

- *Am Wriezener Bahnhof, 10243 Berlin, Germany*
- *+49 30 29360210*

8 BERLIN LOCAL CUISINE

German cuisine features delicious dishes and you can't help but notice that the majority include meat in every form. Whether it's cured or fresh, a dish of beef, pork or goose, it will typically be accompanied by a side of potatoes, carrots, pickles or cabbage. German cuisine is influenced by its neighboring lands and here are some of the typical dishes to try during your trip to Berlin.

Kartoffelsuppe is a savory potato soup that is very popular among the locals of Berlin. **Eisbein**, which literally means ice leg, is a smoked or boiled pork knuckle, is a German dish commonly served with mashed or boiled potatoes. **Senfeir** is another traditional German dish however it doesn't contain meat. The dish is comprised of boiled eggs covered in a mustard sauce and mashed spuds. Senfeir can be enjoyed in almost any restaurant in Berlin.

Wurst is synonymous with Germany and in Berlin you can find wurst at fast food stands, restaurants and of course October Fest. Germany produces an extensive variety of wurst made from beef and pork, each accompanied by a unique sauce.

When it comes to local favorites **Königsberger Klopse** is the real deal; and one of Berlin's most popular comfort foods. In this dish, meatballs are in a creamy sauce of lemon and capers with a side dish of potatoes or rice.

Did you know that "Berliner" translates to "donut" and that it is one of the most abundant sweets found in Berlin? The original version features a yeast dough, filled with marmalade and covered with powdered sugar. Of course, now you can find varieties of the **pfannkuchen**, as they call them in Berlin; decorated with chocolate, delicious icings and flavored doughs.

When it comes to beverages, Germans are known the world over for their love for beer. The brew specific to the capital of Germany is **Berliner Weiße**, a wheat beer with a low percentage of alcohol (only 2,5%). The taste of Berliner Weiße differs from other wheat beers and is rather sour, however it is usually served with a flavored syrup such as raspberry to balance out the sour taste.

What's Cooking in Berlin

If you want to take some cooking classes, one of the recommended schools is **Goldhahn & Sampson**. They host cooking classes a few times a week and you can sign up at http://www.goldhahnundsampson.de/shop/

Cooking classes by **CHEFinBERLIN** can help you learn to prepare vegan gourmet dishes in no time. http://www.chefinberlin.com/CHEFinBERLIN/Welcome.html

If a food tour is what you are after, **Berlin Food Tour** is a place where you can find something for yourself. http://www.berlinfoodtour.de/

9 BERLIN TRAVEL ESSENTIALS

When planning a trip to another country, it is useful to know some practical information that will help make things easier when you arrive. Here are helpful tips you might find useful in Berlin.

Money

As Germany is a part of the European Union, the currency used here is Euro. This same currency can be used in other European countries that are in the EU. When paying for items in Berlin, you can do so in both cash and with credit cards. However, if you are paying in a restaurant or a bar, cash is a more desirable option. Of course, there are banks, exchange offices and ATM machines where you can withdraw or change your money into the currency that you need here.

Phone Calls

If you are dialing Berlin from another European country, dial **00** as the international prefix for calls outside the country, then **49**, which is the country code for Germany and **30**, which is the local area code for Berlin. After that you can enter the rest of the digits to call the number you desire.

The same process is used if you are calling from Berlin; you have to dial **00**, the country code and the local area code for the city you need to call. If you are calling Berlin from the US, dial **011** as the international prefix, **49** for country code and then **30** for local area code.

When you calling from Berlin to the US, it is **00** for the exit, **1** as the country code and the local area code and number.

Standard Mealtimes

When it comes to the standard mealtimes in Germany and Berlin, they don't differ much from the rest of the European countries. Breakfast is usually from 8.00am till 10.00am and the standard time for lunch is between 12.00pm and 2.00pm. The main meal of the day is dinner, which is served usually from 6.00pm till 8.00pm.

Business Hours

Shops are usually open from Monday to Friday from 10.00am to 8.00pm and on some weekends they stay open even longer. All shops, except those on airports are closed on Sundays. Sometimes, there is night shopping and some stores are then open from 1.00pm to 8.00pm. You can find some food late at night at fuel stations. When it comes to the open hours of banks, they usually work from Monday to Friday from 8.00am till 5.00pm, sometimes 6.00pm, and they usually have a break from noon till 1.00pm or 2.00pm.

Key Closure Days

Sunday is almost always a non-working day and shops and some tourist attractions like museums are closed. During the Christmas and Easter holidays and 40 days after Easter (Ascension Day) everything is closed. Other key closure days include May 1st, October 3rd and November 3rd.

10 GERMAN LANGUAGE ESSENTIALS

English speakers will find little issue in communicating with the locals of Berlin. However, if you want to learn some of their essential phrases for directions, a restaurant or a hotel, here is a list to prepare you for your trip to Berlin.

Greetings:

Good day (*formal*) / Guten Tag. (*GOO-ten tahk*)

Good day (*informal*) / Hallo. (Hah-lo)

Goodbye/ Auf Wiedersehen. (*owf VEE-dur-zane*)

Good morning./ Guten Morgen. (*GOO-tun MOR-gun*)

Good evening. / Guten Abend. (*GOO-tun AH-bunt*)

Good night./ Schönen Abend noch. (*shur-nun AH-bunt nokh*)

Good night (*to sleep*)/ Gute Nacht. (*GOO-tuh nakht*)

Directions:

How do I get to _____? (cities)/ Wie komme ich nach _____? (*vee KOM-muh ikh nahkh _____?*)

How do I get to _____? (places, streets)/ Wie komme ich zum/zur _____? (*vee KOM-muh ikh tsoom/tsoor _____?*)

...the train station?/ ...zum Bahnhof? (*tsoom BAHN-hohf?*)

...the bus station / bus stop?/ ...zum Busbahnhof / zur Bushaltestelle? (*tsoom BOOSS-BAHN-hohf/tsoor BOOSS-hahl-tuh-shteh-luh?*)

...the airport?/ ...zum Flughafen? (*tsoom FLOOG-hah-fen?*)

...downtown?/ ...zur Stadtmitte? (*tsoor SHTUT-mit-tuh*)

...the youth hostel?/ ...zur Jugendherberge? (*tsoor YOO-gent-hayr-bayr-guh*)

...the _____ hotel?/ ...zum _____ Hotel? (*tsoom _____ hoh-TELL*)

...the American/Canadian/Australian/British consulate?/ ...zum amerikanischen/kanadischen/australischen/britischen Konsulat? (*tsoom ah-mayr-ih-KAHN-ish-en/kah-NAH-dish-en/ous-TRAH-lish-en/BRIT-ish-en kon-zoo-LAHT?*)

Where are there a lot of.../ Wo gibt es viele... (?) (*VOU gipt ess FEE-luh...*)

...hotels?/ ...Hotels? (*hoh-TELLSS*)

...restaurants?/ ...Restaurants? (*rest-oh-RAHNTS?*)

...sites to see?/ ...Sehenswürdigkeiten? (*ZAY-ens-vuur-dikh-kigh-ten?*)

Can you show me on the map?/ Kannst du/Können Sie mir das auf der Karte zeigen? (*kahnst doo/KOON-en zee meer dahss ouf dayr KAHR-tuh TSIGH-gen?*)

street, road/ Straße (*SHTRAH-suh*)

left/ links (*links*)

right/) rechts (*rekhts*

Turn left./ Links abbiegen. (*LINKS AHP-bee-gen*)

Turn right./ Rechts abbiegen. (*REKHTS AHP-bee-gen*)

straight ahead/ geradeaus (*guh-RAH-duh-OWSS*)

towards the _____/ Richtung _____ (*RIKH-toong*)

past the _____/ nach dem(m)/der(f)/dem(n) _____ (*nahkh daym/dayr/daym* _____)

before the _____/ vor dem(m)/der(f)/dem(n) _____ (*for daym/dayr/daym* _____)

At the Restaurant:

A table for one person/two people, please./ Ein Tisch für eine Person/zwei Personen, bitte. (*ighn TISH fuur IGHN-uh payr-ZOHN/TSVIGH payr-ZOHN-nen, BIT-tuh*)

Can I look at the menu, please?/ Ich hätte gerne die Speisekarte. (*ikh HET-tuh GAYR-nuh dee SHPIGH-zuh-kahr-tuh*)

Is there a house specialty?/ Gibt es eine Spezialität des Hauses? (*gipt ess igh-nuh shpeh-tsyah-lee-TAYT dess HOW-zess?*)

Is there a local specialty?/ Gibt es eine Spezialität aus dieser Gegend? (*gipt ess igh-nuh shpeh-tsyah-lee-TAYT owss DEE-zer GAY-gent?*)

I'm a vegetarian./ Ich bin Vegetarier. (*ikh bin vay-gay-TAH-ree-er*)

I don't eat pork./ Ich esse kein Schweinefleisch. (*ikh ESS-uh kign SHVIGN-uh-flighsh*)

I only eat kosher food./ Ich esse nur koscher. (*ikh ESS-uh noor KOH-sher*)

Can you make it "lite", please? (*less oil/butter/lard*)/ Könnten Sie es bitte nicht so fett machen? (*KOON-ten zee ess BIT-tuh nikht zo fett MAHKH-en?*)

At the Hotel:

Do you have any rooms available?/ Sind noch Zimmer frei? (*ZINT nokh TSIM-mer FRIGH?*)

How much is a room for one person/two people?/ Wie viel kostet ein Einzelzimmer/Doppelzimmer? (*vee-feel KOSS-tet ighn IGHN-tsel-tsim-mer/DOP-pel-tsim-mer?*)

Does the room come with.../ Hat das Zimmer... (*HAHT dahss TSIM-mer...*)

...bedsheets?/ ...Bettlaken? (...*BET-lahk-en?*)

...a bathroom? (toilet)/ ...eine Toilette? (*igh-nuh to-ah-LET-tuh?*)

...a bathroom? (with cleaning facilities)/ ...ein Badezimmer? (*igh-n BAH-duh-tsim-er?*)

...a telephone?/ ...ein Telefon? (*ighn tell-eh-FOHN?*)

...a TV?/ ...einen Fernseher? (*igh-nen FAYRN-zay-er?*)

May I see the room first?/ Kann ich das Zimmer erstmal sehen? (*kahn ikh dahs TSIM-mer ayrst-mahl ZAY-en?*)

Do you have anything quieter?/ Haben Sie etwas Ruhigeres? (*HAH-ben zee ET-vahs ROO-ig-er-ess?*)

...bigger?/ ...größeres? (*GROO-ser-ess?*)

...cheaper?/ ...billigeres? (*BILL-ig-er-ess?*)

OK, I'll take it./ OK, ich nehme es. (*OH-kay, ikh NAY-muh ess*)

I will stay for _____ night(s)./ Ich bleibe eine Nacht (_____ Nächte). (*ihk BLIGH-buh IGH-nuh* *nahkht/_____ NEKH-tuh*) **Note:***The plural of* Nacht' *is* 'Nächte'.

Social:

How are you? (*used as a real question, not a form of greeting.*)/ Wie geht's? (*vee GATES?*)

Fine, thank you./ Gut, danke. (*goot, DAN-keh*)

What is your name? (*formal*)/ Wie heißen Sie? (*vee HIGH-sun zee?*)

What is your name? (*informal*)/ Wie heißt du? (*vee HIGHST doo?*)

My name is _____ ./ Ich heiße _____ . (*eesh HIGH-suh*)

Nice to meet you. (formal)/ Nett, Sie kennen zu lernen. (*net zee KEN-en tsoo LER-nen*)

Nice to meet you. (informal)/ Nett, dich kennen zu lernen. (*net deesh KEN-en tsoo LER-nen*)

Please./ Bitte. (*BEE-tuh*)

Thank you./ Danke schön. (*DAN-kuh shurn*)

Thanks./ Danke. (*DAN-kuh*)

You're welcome./ Bitte schön! (*BEE-tuh shurn*)

Yes./ Ja. (*yah*)

No./ Nein. (*nine*)

Excuse me. (*getting attention*)/ Entschuldigen Sie. (*ent-SHOOL-dee-gun zee*)

Excuse me. (*begging pardon*)/ Entschuldigung. (*ent-SHOOL-dee-goong*)

I'm sorry./ Es tut mir leid. (*es toot meer lite*)

I can't speak German (well)./ Ich kann nicht [so gut] Deutsch sprechen. (*eesh kahn nikht [zo goot] doytsh shprekhen*)

Do you speak English? (formal)/ Sprechen Sie Englisch? (*shprekhun zee ENG-leesh*)

Is there someone here who speaks English?/ Gibt es hier jemanden, der Englisch spricht? (*geept es heer yeh-MAHN-dun dare ENG-leesh shprikht*)

11 BERLIN TOP 20 THINGS TO DO

As the capital of Germany, Berlin is a city that offers visitors plenty of interesting things to do. Many can be found right in the city and others nearby. Here are the top 20 things in Berlin that you should not miss.

Brandenburg Gate is one of the symbols of Berlin that you will find on many postcards. This imposing gate located in the Unter den Linden Avenue was built as the entrance to the city that lead to the royal palace in the 18th century. No one should return from Berlin without taking a photo in front of this iconic building.

http://www.berlin.de/orte/sehenswuerdigkeiten/brandenburger-tor/index.en.php

Berlin Cathedral is the biggest city church and another recognizable symbol of Berlin. It was not alwys like thies, even though the history of this church goes back to the mid 15th century. It is located in the Am Lustgarten and the surrounding is alsobeautiful, but not near as the cathedral itself.

http://www.berlinerdom.de/?lang=en

Checkpoint Charlie is a symbol of the turbulent history of Germany and represents a period when the Berlin wall divided East and West Berlin. It was a time when citizens could only venture to the other side of the wall with special permissions. It is located in the Friedrichstrasse, near the Topography of Terror.

East Side Gallery is also a part of the history connected to the Berlin Wall. It is actually a part of the Berlin Wall that was decorated with graffiti and turned into one of the largest open galleries in the world. It is located in the Muehlenstrasse, near the Spree River.

http://www.eastsidegallery-berlin.de/

Museuminsel is a unique complex of 5 museums located on the North side of the river Spree and near the Berlin Cathedral. Museums are also near the Royal Palace, which is not by coincidence as the Royal family were the ones who wanted to build this complex, and many artifacts are from their private collection.

https://www.berlin.de/orte/sehenswuerdigkeiten/museumsinsel/index.en.php

Charlottenburg Palace was built in 1699 as a summer residence for Sophie Charlotte, wife of king Frederick XI. It is an amazing edifice located in Spandauer Damm, but the only way you can visit it is in an organized tour. The beautiful galleries feature a stunning colleciton of Picasso's artwork.

http://www.spsg.de/startseite/

Deutscher Dom is one of the two churches located at Gendarmer Markt, a beautiful square in Berlin. The church is in the South part of the square, and on the South is a nearly identical church, Französischer Dom.

http://www.berlin.de/en/museums/3109333-3104050-deutscher-dom.en.html

Potsdam Gardens is located just outside of Berlin. You will need a whole day if you want to fully enjoy their beauty and see the palaces scattered around. The gardens are located in Schopenhauerstrasse, Potsdam, about a 20 min. of drive from Berlin.

http://www.potsdam-tourism.com/highlights.html

Olympic Stadium is another reminder of the Nazi history in Germany. It was built for Olympic Games in 1936. Outstanding both from the inside-out, this monumental attraction in Berlin is located at the Olympischer Platz 3. Admission is around 10€.

http://www.olympiastadion-berlin.de/en.html

The Holocaust Memorial is located near the Brandenburg Gate, making it very easy to find it. It is an important historical site that represents the suffering of Jews in the WW II. There is also a museum under the memorial where you can uncover even more historical information.

http://www.holocaust-mahnmal.de/en/home.html

Topography of Terror is a place where the headquarters during the "Third Reich" were located and there is now an exhibition where you can view photos, articles from newspapers and other documents from the period. It is located at Niederkirchnerstrasse, near Checkpoint Charlie.

http://www.topographie.de/en/

Mauerpark is a paradise for those who like shopping. The park features a large flea market where you can buy literally everything. After 3.00pm there is a karaoke show where everyone; young, old, residents and tourists, have an opportunity to sing.

http://www.flohmarktimmauerpark.de/

TV Tower is the highest point from which you can see a panoramic of Berlin. It is 207m high and includes a restaurant that revolves making it an ideal choice for a lovely dinner with a view at Berlin's attractions. It is located at Alexanderplatz where you can also view Neptune's Fountain.

https://www.tv-turm.de/en/

Victory Column is another great site surrounded by a beautiful park in Am Grossen Stern. It was built in the 19th century as a symbol of Prussia's victory in the Franco-German war. There are 207 stairs that lead to the top which you can venture up with paid admission.

http://www.berlin.de/orte/sehenswuerdigkeiten/siegessaeule/

Concert Hall is now a host of numerous cultural events and concerts. It was re-opened in 1984 after renewal from the damage caused by the attacks during the WW II. It is located at Gendarmenmarkt.

http://en.konzerthaus.de/

Treptower Park is located in Puschkinallee, on a hill outside the buzz of the city hosts an enormous statue dedicated to the Russian soldiers that died in the battle for Berlin. It is an off the beaten path location, but worth visiting.

http://www.visitberlin.de/en/spot/treptow-park

Bode Museum is located at Bodestrasse and showcases beautiful architecture along with varied collections and artworks. Inside you will find a café where you can take a break and enjoy a cup of coffee during your trip. It is open from 10.00am to 6.00pm on Tuesday, Thursday and Friday.

http://www.smb.museum/en/museums-and-institutions/bode-museum/home.html

Reichstag is the building where the German Parliament is situated. It is located near the Brandenburg gate, at the Platz der Republik. Besides housing the German Parliament, it is also another German building with stunning architecture.

http://www.bundestag.de/

Tier Garten is a real gem near the center of Berlin. You can enjoy long walks, have a dinner in one of the restaurants and view interesting statues and monuments. It's a wholesome slice of nature in the city and is located on Strasse des 17. Juni.

http://www.berlin.de/orte/sehenswuerdigkeiten/tiergarten/index.en.php?lang=en

Gendarmenmarkt is a town square in Berlin surrounded by several historical building and sites. It is also known as a place for shopping, as well as a prime destination for those who love architecture and history. Gendarmenmarkt is located in Mitte.

https://www.berlin.de/orte/sehenswuerdigkeiten/gendarmenmarkt/index.en.php?lang=en

CONCLUSION

What to expect of this trip?

If you have ever dreamt of travelling through space and time, by choosing to go to Berlin you have taken a step in the right direction, as the German capital and cultural center is more of a time-machine than simply a city. Nonetheless, Berlin is not just a place of grand architecture, it is also home to some of the most creative and impressive artistic expressions in the world. So, if you have decided to spend a few days in the capital, prepare to be inspired and awed.

MORE FROM THIS AUTHOR

Below you'll find some of our other books that are popular on Amazon and Kindle as well. Alternatively, you can visit our author page on Amazon to see other work done by us.

3 Day Guide to Berlin: A 72-hour definitive guide on what to see, eat and enjoy in Berlin, Germany

3 Day Guide to Vienna: A 72-hour definitive guide on what to see, eat and enjoy in Vienna Austria

3 Day Guide to Santorini: A 72-hour definitive guide on what to see, eat and enjoy in Santorini Greece

3 Day Guide to Provence: A 72-hour definitive guide on what to see, eat and enjoy in Provence, France

3 Day Guide to Istanbul: A 72-hour definitive guide on what to see, eat and enjoy in Istanbul, Turkey

3 Day Guide to Budapest: A 72-hour Definitive Guide on What to See, Eat and Enjoy in Budapest, Hungary

3 Day Guide to Venice: A 72-hour Definitive Guide on What to See, Eat and Enjoy in Venice, Italy

# 3 DAY CITY GUIDES